D0207183

Molière's Tartuffe; or, The Imposter

Translated by

Christopher Hampton

S A M U E L   F R E N C H ,   I N C .
45 WEST 25TH STREET   NEW YORK 10010
7623 SUNSET BOULEVARD   HOLLYWOOD 90046
LONDON   TORONTO

A Note on the Text

The text published here is a translation of the complete Molière play. For various reasons, it differs in minor ways from the text played by the Royal Shakespeare Company. First, some small cuts were made in our production, which sometimes necessitated alterations in order to preserve the metre; secondly, Bill Alexander's decision to set the play in a dining-room, rather than in the anonymous *salle basse* referred to in Act Three, required some occasional adjustments, not preserved here; and, finally, I have incorporated some second thoughts of my own, arrived at since the production opened.

A word about Tartuffe's servant, the mysterious Laurent. This character is not included in Molière's *dramatis personae*: but the layout of French classical plays calls for a new scene at the appearance of each new character and lists the characters at the head of each scene—and at the head of Act Three, Scene 2, is found the name of Laurent. Acting on this hint, and on Orgon's description of him as Tartuffe's 'mirror-image', we introduced Laurent in a number of other scenes in the play; and indeed in the final scene, without changing the text, the Officer managed to indicate, by a resourceful use of the personal pronoun, that it was Laurent who had betrayed Tartuffe to the King. That Tartuffe's pupil has learnt from him the rewards of judicious treachery, is perhaps more likely than that the King, in addition to all his other virtues, is a master detective. In any event, I pass it on as what seems to me one of the production's happiest inventions.

C.H.

A Note on the Translation

The verse plays of Molière are traditionally translated either into prose or into rhymed iambic pentameter (and never, as far as I know, into their own metre, the dodecasyllabic Alexandrine of the French classical theatre, so memorably disposed of by Pope in his description of the 'needless Alexandrine', 'that like a wounded snake, drags its slow length along'). Since Molière also wrote prose plays, in which the tone was less formal, the language racier and the adjectives fewer, translation into prose, whatever its advantages in conveying Molière's invariable lucidity, would seem to be something of an evasion. With translations into rhyming verse, the difficulties lie elsewhere. The French language has a much more rigid and defined phonetic structure than English; and when one takes into account, additionally, the inflected endings, the regular participial formations, the silent plurals and the verb forms, whether infinitive or conjugated, it will be clear that the business of finding a rhyme is infinitely simpler and more natural in French than it can ever be in English. There have been a number of admirable rhyming translations of Molière: but the ingenuity they demand cannot avoid drawing attention to itself, somewhat at the expense of the line of the play as a whole. It's impossible to imagine, for example, a rhyme in a Molière play causing laughter *in itself*, a common effect in good English rhymed translations.

For these and other reasons, it seemed to me logical to translate a play written in Alexandrines, the form naturally adopted by dramatists in the golden age of French theatre, into the form adopted equally naturally by English dramatists in their golden age: namely blank verse. My iambics are rougher and less regular than Molière's Alexandrines; but a certain insouciance he has with syllable counts shows him to be not entirely comfortable within the confines of the form. In any event, it's a long time since I first expressed this theory of how Molière's verse plays might be translated: and I'm grateful to the Royal Shakespeare Company for inviting me to put it into practice.

C.H.

A Note on the Play

The *Tartuffe* we know is the third distinct version of a play which had to wait five years before it was licensed for public performance by the King. To say that during that time it had become a *cause célèbre* would be something of an understatement: its underground reputation had spread so far afield that Queen Christina of Sweden had sent for a copy and applied (unsuccessfully) for permission to have it performed; while various respectable clerics, with or without benefit of having read the play, did not hesitate to demand that its author be burnt at the stake.

The two earlier versions of the play are unfortunately lost to us: all we do know for certain is that the first version, when it was privately performed for the King in 1664, was in three acts as opposed to five and was called *Tartuffe ou l'Hypocrite*. John Cairncross has painstakingly and convincingly deduced* that this first version consisted, by and large, of Acts One, Three and Four of the present text, ending perhaps (given Molière's classical taste for symmetry) with the Mme Pernelle scene from Act Five. Be that as it may, what is remarkable is that the finished *Tartuffe* seems so tightly constructed, showing none of the joins such a complicated process of reconstruction, expansion and compromise must have necessitated.

Small wonder that the play ends with the famous panegyric to Louis XIV for preserving not only Orgon and his family but the very existence of the play itself. And certainly when *Tartuffe* at last opened to the public on 5 February 1669 the vicissitudes of its composition in no way harmed its success: it played for an unprecedented twenty-eight consecutive performances and subsequently became (with around 3,000 performances at the Comédie-Française alone) the most frequently produced play in the French language.

C.H.

*John Cairncross, *New Light on Molière*, Droz/Minard, 1956.

Characters

MADAME PERNELLE, Orgon's mother
ORGON, Elmire's husband
ELMIRE, Orgon's wife
DAMIS, Orgon's son
MARIANE, Orgon's daughter, in love with Valère
VALÈRE, in love with Mariane
CLÉANTE, Orgon's brother-in-law
TARTUFFE, a hypocrite
DORINE, Mariane's maid
MONSIEUR LOYAL, a bailiff
AN OFFICER
FLIPOTE, Mme Pernelle's maidservant
LAURENT, Tartuffe's manservant

The play is set in Paris, in Orgon's house.

Tartuffe or The Impostor, translated by Christopher Hampton, was first performed at The Pit, London, on 20 July 1983. The cast was as follows:

MADAME PERNELLE	Sylvia Coleridge
ORGON	Nigel Hawthorne
ELMIRE	Alison Steadman
DAMIS	Mark Rylance
MARIANE	Katy Behean
VALÈRE	Ian Talbot
CLÉANTE	David Bradley
TARTUFFE	Antony Sher
DORINE	Stephanie Fayerman
MONSIEUR LOYAL	Robin Meredith
OFFICER	David Glover
FLIPOTE	Sara Mair-Thomas
LAURENT	John Tramper

Directed by Bill Alexander
Designed by Alison Chitty
Lighting by Leo Leibovici

ACT ONE

SCENE ONE

MADAME PERNELLE, *her maidservant* FLIPOTE, ELMIRE, MARIANE, DORINE, DAMIS, CLÉANTE.

MME PERNELLE:	Come on, Flipote, let's go, I can't stay here.
ELMIRE:	Why are you in such a rush? We can't keep up.
MME PERNELLE:	Then leave me, dear, don't take another step.
	I'm sure I never asked for all this fuss.
ELMIRE:	I think we know our duty and we'll do it.
	But what is it that's made you run away?
MME PERNELLE:	I can't bear all the turmoil in this house.
	Nobody cares a button for my feelings.
	It's been a most unedifying visit:
	nobody listens to a word I say;
	there's no respect, everyone shouts at once,
	it's like some frightful Parliament of Apes.
DORINE:	If . . .
MME PERNELLE:	You, my girl, are nothing but a maid
	with far too much to say and most of that
	impertinent; we don't need your opinion.
DAMIS:	But . . .
MME PERNELLE:	There's a word for you, my boy:
	buffoon.
	Yes, I'm your grandmother and I should know.
	And if I've told your father once, I've told him
	a hundred times, I think you're a bad lot,
	who'll never give him anything but heartache.
MARIANE:	I think . . .
MME PERNELLE:	Good Lord, the quiet one's found
	her voice,
	sweetness and light, the sister meek and mild;
	but still waters run deep, they always say,
	and deep down you're as bad as all the rest.

ELMIRE:	But, mother . . .
MME PERNELLE:	Now, dear, don't take this amiss,
	but everything you do is simply wrong.
	You ought to set these two a good example,
	as their late mother never failed to do.
	You spend too much, I must say it upsets me,
	the way you go round dressed like a princess.
	A woman who wants just to please her husband
	has no business parading like a clothes-horse.
CLÉANTE:	But, after all, Madame . . .
MME PERNELLE:	And as for you,
	it's not that I don't like you and respect you,
	but if I were my son's wife, even if
	you were my brother, you'd be barred the house:
	spouting your endless theories about life,
	which no one in their right mind would accept.
	Perhaps I've been too frank; but I'm like that,
	I never could conceal what's on my mind.
DAMIS:	I'm sure your Monsieur Tartuffe would be pleased . . .
MME PERNELLE:	He's a good man, who must be listened to,
	and if I have to hear a fool like you
	attacking him, I may get very cross.
DAMIS:	Some sanctimonious faker seizes power,
	and I'm supposed to lie back and enjoy it,
	and no one is allowed the simplest pleasure
	without permission from this turkey-cock!
DORINE:	If what he says is anything to go by,
	you move and you commit a mortal sin:
	his beady critic's eye is watching you.
MME PERNELLE:	And everything he watches must be watched.
	He's trying to lead you up the path to Heaven,
	and my son ought to force you all to love him.
DAMIS:	No, listen to me, grandmother, no father,
	no anyone could make me wish him well.

	If I said otherwise, I would be lying.

If I said otherwise, I would be lying.
The way he carries on infuriates me.
There's only one way out of this, I tell you,
I and that peasant can't but come to blows.

DORINE: You can't deny it's scandalous to see
a stranger taking over here, a beggar
who, when he came, had nothing on his feet
and whose whole wardrobe wasn't worth a
                                              fiver,
going so far as to forget his place,
lording it over us and finding fault.

MME PERNELLE: Good gracious me, you'd all be better off,
if you submitted to his pious will!

DORINE: You have this fantasy that he's a saint,
when everything he does proves he's a fraud.

MME PERNELLE: Be quiet!

DORINE: I'd need a written guarantee,
before I'd trust him or his man Laurent.

MME PERNELLE: I can't vouch for his servant, but Tartuffe
—you have my guarantee he's a good man.
The only reason you object to him
is that his criticisms are all true.
What makes him angry is your sinfulness,
his sole criterion is what's good for Heaven.

DORINE: I know, but why, especially recently,
is he so very down on visitors?
He makes so much fuss, it gives you a
                                         headache.
What harm's a courtesy visit do to Heaven?
You want my explanation? Keep it quiet,
(*She turns to* ELMIRE.)
but I'm convinced he's jealous of your friends.

MME PERNELLE: You shut your mouth and think before you
                                                   speak.
He's not the only one who disapproves:
it's all the fuss your visitors bring with them,
carriages always blocking up the gates,

vast quantities of footmen milling round,
making a noise and upsetting the neighbours.
I'm willing to believe nothing goes on;
but people talk, and that's to be avoided.

CLÉANTE: And how do you propose to stop them talking?
Life would be pretty miserable if,
for fear of what some imbecile might say,
you had to give up all your closest friends.
And even if you did decide to do that,
you think you'd put a stop to all the rumours?
There's no defence against malicious talk.
So let's pay no attention to it, please,
let's live as blamelessly as we can manage
and leave the gossips to say what they like.

DORINE: I know who runs us down behind our backs,
it's Daphné, next door, and the dwarf, her
husband.
It's always the most ludicrously guilty,
who are the first in line accusing others.
They never miss an opportunity
to batten on the slightest hint of friendship,
twist it to suit their purposes and then
gleefully spread the news to everyone.
They think they justify their own misconduct
by painting others' deeds in lurid colours,
and hope, in vain, to whitewash their intrigues,
or to sidestep the general condemnation
which weighs them down and redistribute it.

MME PERNELLE: Your arguments are quite irrelevant.
Orante, who's well known for her model life
and pious dedication, says, I hear,
she strongly disapproves of your salon.

DORINE: Well, she's a fine example, I must say!
She may personify austerity,
but what inspires her zeal is called old age.
She's virtuous because she has no choice.
As long as she was still at all attractive,

she made the most of everything she had;
but now the sparkle in her eye has dimmed,
she's registering withdrawal from the world
before it casts her off, and trying to hide
the sorry remnants of her faded beauty
behind an ornate veil of good behaviour.
These are the standard wiles of ageing flirts.
It's hard for them to watch their beaux
disperse.
And so the only outlet for their suffering
is to take virtue up professionally;
and the puritan code of these good ladies
implacably finds fault with everything.
They disapprove of everybody's life,
not from benevolence but spurred by envy:
they just can't tolerate the thought of pleasures,
which the onset of age denies to them.

MME PERNELLE: (*To* ELMIRE)
You all enjoy these fairytales, I see.
In your house no one gets a word in edgeways,
because of madam holding forth all day;
well, now I've got a chance to speak at last,
I'm telling you, the wisest thing my son
has ever done is to install Tartuffe,
whom God has sent here, just when he was
needed,
to save your souls, when you had gone astray;
listen to what he says, it's for your good,
everything he condemns deserves condemning.
These visitors, these dances, these discussions
—all of them are inventions of the devil;
you never hear a word about religion,
just idle chatter, songs, that sort of nonsense,
often as not demolishing your neighbours
and spreading slanders left and right, until
sensible people's heads are spinning with it,
dozens of rumours whipped up out of nothing,

and as a friend of mine, theologist,
put it so pithily the other day:
in the Tower of Babel, babble's what you get,
and he went on to illustrate his point . . .
(*She indicates* CLÉANTE.)
I don't know what he's sniggering about.
Go to an asylum if you want to laugh
and don't . . .
(*To* ELMIRE)
          I'll say no more. Goodbye, my
                          dear,
I take a very poor view of all this.
You won't be seeing me for quite some time.
(*She slaps* FLIPOTE.)
Well, come along, wake up, don't gawk at me!
My goodness me, I'll box your ears for you.
Get on with you, you slut!

SCENE TWO

CLÉANTE, DORINE.

CLÉANTE: I'm staying put,
I don't want her to start on me again.
Silly old . . .

DORINE: What a shame she isn't here
to comment on your turn of phrase: I know
she'd tell you you're the one who's being silly
and that no one could ever call her old.

CLÉANTE: She got annoyed with us for no good reason,
and she seems quite besotted with Tartuffe!

DORINE: I promise you her son is even worse
and if you saw him you would be appalled.
During the troubles he was very brave,
enhanced his reputation with the King,

but ever since he's fallen for Tartuffe,
he's gone around like someone in a daze.
He loves the man: a hundred times as much as
his wife, his son, his daughter or his mother;
he calls him brother, whispers all his secrets
to him alone and has appointed him
the watchful overseer of his conduct.
He pampers him, caresses him: I'd say
you couldn't be more loving to a mistress.
He sits him at the top end of the table,
enjoys watching him eat enough for six;
you have to serve him all the tastiest bits,
and even when he burps, he says: 'God bless
                                       you!'
In short, he's mad about him; he's his hero,
his everything, admired in every way
and quoted on all possible occasions,
his slightest action is miraculous
and every word he says is like an oracle.
The fact is, he's a man can spot a victim
and knows how to exploit and dazzle him
with every bogus swindle in the book.
He wheedles money when he feels like it,
by turning on his sanctimonious cant
and doesn't hesitate to pick on us.
Even his servant orders us about,
gives himself airs and preaches wild-eyed sermons
and throws away our rouge and beauty spots.
The other day the brute found my lace bib
between two pages of *The Lives of the Saints*
and ripped it up, saying it was a crime
to stain what's holy with the devil's frills.

SCENE THREE

ELMIRE, MARIANE, DAMIS, CLÉANTE, DORINE.

ELMIRE: (*To* CLÉANTE)
You're very wise to have stayed here, you
missed
her lecture at the gate. My husband's here:
he hasn't seen me and I'd rather wait
for him upstairs.

CLÉANTE: I'll wait and catch him here,
I've really only time to say hello.

DAMIS: Ask him about my sister's wedding, will you?
I have a feeling Tartuffe is against it
and forcing him to make these long delays.
It's important to me as well, you know.
My sister loves Valère and he loves her:
but, as you know, I'm in love with his sister,
and if . . .

DORINE: He's coming.

SCENE FOUR

ORGON, CLÉANTE, DORINE.

ORGON: Ah, Cléante, hello!

CLÉANTE: I was just on my way, I'm glad I caught you.
Nothing much out yet, is there, in the country?

ORGON: Dorine . . .
(*To* CLÉANTE)

You must excuse me, just a minute,
you don't mind if I find out what's been

happening

and put my mind at rest?
(*To* DORINE)

Everything fine?

What's everybody up to? Are they well?

DORINE: Two days ago the mistress had a fever
and a strange nagging headache all day long.

ORGON: And Tartuffe?

DORINE: Tartuffe's in the best of health,
big, fat and blooming, with his nice red mouth.

ORGON: Poor boy!

DORINE: She felt quite nauseous all evening
and couldn't touch a mouthful of her dinner,
her headache was so painful.

ORGON: And Tartuffe?

DORINE: He sat in front of her and ate alone,
swallowing, most religiously, a brace
of partridge, followed by a leg of mutton.

ORGON: Poor boy!

DORINE: She never closed her eyes all night,
she had hot flushes, which kept her awake,
we had to sit up with her till the dawn.

ORGON: And Tartuffe?

DORINE: He was struck down by a kind

of

pleasantly weary feeling and repaired
directly from the table to his room,
where he collapsed into his nice warm bed
and slumbered dreamlessly until the morning.

ORGON: Poor boy!

DORINE: We finally persuaded her
to be bled, and she felt better at once.

ORGON: And Tartuffe?

DORINE: Put his bravest face on it,
and, bracing himself against the blows of fate,

17

> to make up for the blood the mistress lost,
> drank four large tumblersful of wine for
> > breakfast.

ORGON: Poor boy!

DORINE: At any rate they're now quite well,
and I must go upstairs and tell the mistress
how interested you've been in her recovery.

SCENE FIVE

ORGON, CLÉANTE.

CLÉANTE: She's making fun of you, you must have
> noticed;
and I don't want to make you angry, but,
quite frankly, it's no more than you deserve.
I've never heard of such grotesque behaviour:
how can this man have cast a spell and made
> you
oblivious to everybody else?
So that as well as saving him from poverty,
you've gone as far as to . . .

ORGON: That's quite
> enough!
How can you talk about him, you don't know
> him.

CLÉANTE: Certainly I don't know him, but to guess
the kind of man he is, you only need to . . .

ORGON: No, you'd be captivated by him, and
your ecstasy would know no bounds. You see,
this is a man, who . . . well . . . a man in
> fact . . .
er, to sum up, a man. You listen to him
and you enjoy the deepest peace of mind
and see the world for what it is: a dunghill.

18

Oh, yes, I've quite changed under his
                                    instruction:
he teaches me to cast aside affection
and clear my mind of any trace of love;
now I could watch my mother or my brother,
my wife and children die, and not give that.

CLÉANTE: I see, he's a humanitarian.

ORGON: Ah, if you'd only been there when we met,
you'd feel as warm towards him as I do.
He'd arrive every day in church and kneel,
meekly, right next to me and never fail
to capture the whole congregation's notice
with the enthusiasm of his praying;
he'd groan and sigh and throw himself around
and humbly kiss the ground, time and again,
and when I left, he'd hurry on ahead
to hand me the holy water at the door.
His servant, who was like his mirror image,
told me about him, who he was, his poverty:
I gave him money; but, restrained as ever,
he always tried to give some back to me.
'Too much,' he'd say, 'I don't need half this
                                    much,
What makes you think I should deserve your
                                    pity?'
When I'd refuse to take it back, he'd go
and share it with the poor, in front of me.
Finally I was inspired to bring him here,
since when it seems that all of us have
                                    flourished.
He disapproves of everything, of course,
and keeps a very close watch on my wife,
just to protect my honour; gives me names
of all the people who make eyes at her;
he's far more jealous than I've ever been.
You've no idea, the fervour of the man:
he sees the slightest failing as a sin,

	he's scandalized by what we'd hardly notice;

he's scandalized by what we'd hardly notice;
recently he was full of self-reproach
for having caught a flea while he was praying
and killed it with excessive savagery.

CLÉANTE: What is this, are you making fun of me?
You must be mad, you think this
pantomime . . .

ORGON: Now, what you're saying smacks of atheism.
You're tainted with it, and if I've told you
once,
I've told you fifty times, that's the best way
to get yourself into quite serious trouble.

CLÉANTE: I know, that's what you people always say.
You want us all to be as blind as you are.
Good eyesight is a sign of atheism,
and anyone who doesn't worship idols
has no respect and no religious faith.
Nothing you say can frighten me: God sees
into my heart and I know what I mean.
You can't make me a slave of affectation:
false piety's as common as false courage,
and just as on the battlefield you find
that those who make the loudest noise are not
the truly brave, the truly pious, whose
example we should follow, equally,
are not the ones who pull the holiest faces.
Can it be true you don't make a distinction
between hypocrisy and piety?
And do you really class them both together,
respect the mask as highly as the face,
consider sham the equal of sincerity,
confuse appearance and reality,
value a ghost as much as someone living
and forgeries no less than genuine coin?
Men are peculiar creatures, most of them!
They never seem to hit the happy medium.
Reason's too limited, they burst its bounds,

and often what's most admirable's ruined
through sheer exaggeration and excess.
I only thought I'd mention this in passing.

ORGON: Yes, I see, you're a most distinguished genius,
repository of universal knowledge,
uniquely brilliant and uniquely wise,
an oracle, a Cato of our time,
compared to whom the rest of us are fools.

CLÉANTE: No, I am not a most distinguished genius,
repository of universal knowledge:
but there's one thing I do know how to do,
that's tell the difference between true and false.
And while there's no one I approve of more
than genuinely religious men, and nothing
nobler or more uplifting in the world
than the enthusiasm of true belief,
equally, there is nothing more disgraceful
than specious fervour laid on with a trowel,
and no one worse than those downright
                                       impostors,
those worshippers in public, whose deceit
and sacreligious antics go unpunished,
while they pervert and make a mockery of
everything human beings hold most sacred;
those career mystics, businessmen on their
                                        knees,
trying to notch up credit and prestige,
by screwing up their eyes and throwing fits;
those abnormally zealous ones, I mean,
chasing their fortunes via the road to Heaven,
who make demands between each ardent
                                        prayer,
and make sure they are well installed at Court
before they preach withdrawal from the world,
whose faith's adjustable to fit their vices,
who are disloyal, fleet, vindictive, cunning,
and, when the time comes to destroy an enemy,

can brazenly disguise their fierce resentments
behind a cover of what's good for Heaven;
doubly dangerous because the weapons
they turn against us in their bitterness
are so respected, and because the passion,
for which they are so genuinely admired,
aims at our hearts a consecrated sword.
This faking is becoming far too common;
meanwhile our age has shown us, very often,
glorious examples of true piety,
easily recognizable as such.
Look at Ariston, look at Périandre,
Oronte, Alcidamas, Polydore, Clitandre:
no one disputes their genuineness, and yet
none of them ever boasts about his virtue
or displays such intolerable pride,
their religion is flexible and humane.
They're not censorious, because that would
                                      show
an arrogance they'd rather leave to others,
if they reproach us, then it's through their
                                      actions.
They don't judge by appearances, instead
their inclination's to think well of others.
They don't form cliques, they don't approve of
                                      plotting:
their only aim is to live righteously.
They have no animosity against sinners,
reserving all their hatred for the sin,
and no urge to pursue the Church's interests
more violently than it would itself.
They're the ones I approve of, that's the way,
that's the example one should set oneself.
Frankly, your man is quite another species;
I'm sure you sing his praises in good faith,
but I believe you're blinded by mere show.

ORGON: Is that all?

CLÉANTE:	Yes.
ORGON:	Then perhaps you would excuse me?

(He makes to go.)

CLÉANTE:	Oh, just one minute, please: I'll change the subject. You have promised Valère your daughter's hand?
ORGON:	Yes.
CLÉANTE:	And you'd even given them a date?
ORGON:	That's right.
CLÉANTE:	Then why have you postponed the wedding?
ORGON:	I've no idea.
CLÉANTE:	Have you perhaps changed your mind?
ORGON:	Possibly.
CLÉANTE:	Are you going to break your word?
ORGON:	I didn't say that.
CLÉANTE:	I just can't imagine what could prevent you honouring your promise.
ORGON:	Depends.
CLÉANTE:	What is all this evasiveness? Valère has asked me to see you about it.
ORGON:	Well, that is nice.
CLÉANTE:	But what am I to tell him?
ORGON:	You tell him what you like.
CLÉANTE:	But then I have to know what you have in mind: what are your plans?
ORGON:	To do God's will.
CLÉANTE:	Be serious, will you? Look: Valère has had your promise: will you keep it?
ORGON:	Goodbye.
CLÉANTE:	*(Alone)* I fear the worst for his engagement. I have to warn him of what's going on.

ACT TWO

SCENE ONE

ORGON, MARIANE.

ORGON: Mariane.

MARIANE: Yes, father.

ORGON: Come here, I'd like
a word with you in private.

MARIANE: What's in there?

(ORGON *is looking into a closet*.)

ORGON: Nothing, I'm only checking no one's there,
I wouldn't like us to be overheard.
No, that's all right. Well, Mariane, I've always
appreciated your obedience,
and you've always been very dear to me.

MARIANE: I'm very grateful, father, that you love me.

ORGON: Well said, my dear. And if I'm to continue,
your only worry need be to provide me
with what I want.

MARIANE: I take a pride in it.

ORGON: Good. What do you think of our guest,
Tartuffe?

MARIANE: Who, me?

ORGON: You. Now, be careful what you say.

MARIANE: Oh, dear. Well, I'll say anything you like.

ORGON: How very sensible. Well, then, my dear,
why don't you say he's wholly excellent,
he's reached your heart and it would make you
happy
if I agreed to let him marry you?
Mm?

(MARIANE *steps back, surprised*.)

MARIANE: Mm?

ORGON: What is it?

25

MARIANE:	Sorry?
ORGON:	What?
MARIANE:	I don't think I caught what you said.
ORGON:	What do you mean?
MARIANE:	Who is it that you wanted me to say had reached my heart? And it would make me happy if you agreed to let me marry whom?
ORGON:	Tartuffe.
MARIANE:	But, look, it wouldn't, not at all. Why should you want to make me tell a lie?
ORGON:	What I want is for it to be the truth; that's my decision, what more do you need?
MARIANE:	You mean you want . . .
ORGON:	Yes, my dear, I intend to make Tartuffe a member of the family. He's going to be your husband, it's all settled, and since I have the power to insist . . .

SCENE TWO

DORINE, ORGON, MARIANE.
ORGON *notices* DORINE.

ORGON:	What are you doing? Eavesdropping again? Suffering from chronic curiosity?
DORINE:	I heard somebody mentioning this marriage, and I couldn't decide if it was rumour, with some basis in fact, or pure invention: the one obvious thing was it was nonsense.
ORGON:	You find it unbelievable?

DORINE:	So much so, I wouldn't believe it, even if you told me.
ORGON:	I think I know a way to make you, though.
DORINE:	I know, you're telling us a fairy story.
ORGON:	I'm telling you exactly what will happen.
DORINE:	Rubbish!
ORGON:	Now, this is serious, Mariane.
DORINE:	Get on with you, your father doesn't mean it, he's joking.
ORGON:	Will you listen . . . ?
DORINE:	No, no good, we don't believe you.
ORGON:	I'm starting to get annoyed.
DORINE:	All right, we do believe you, then. In which case, shame on you. You look quite normal, that big beard in the middle of your face, and yet you mean you're mad enough to . . .
ORGON:	Listen: you've taken certain liberties today which I don't like one little bit: I warn you . . .
DORINE:	Let's try and keep our temper, shall we, sir? I still think this is some elaborate joke. Your daughter isn't cut out for a bigot, and he should have other things on his mind. And anyway, what possible advantage could such a marriage bring you? And why choose a beggar for a son-in-law with all your money . . . ?
ORGON:	That's enough. If he has nothing, all the more reason to admire him. His poverty is honest poverty: it lifts him higher than the great, he's poor through voluntary renunciation and

his pure indifference to temporal things
and his commitment to eternity.
I intend to provide him with some means,
free him from want and re-acquire his lands,
properties highly thought of where he comes
                                         from;
even as he stands, it's obvious he's a
                                    gentleman.

DORINE: So he keeps saying, and that kind of pride
doesn't quite fit with his religiousness.
You wouldn't think a man who'd chosen
                                  sainthood
would need to boast about his name and rank;
the self-effacing rules of piety
hardly accommodate rampant ambition.
What is the purpose of his vanity . . . ?
This is upsetting you: let's leave his
                               background
and talk about his personality.
Could you really, without the least remorse,
hand a girl like her to a man like him?
Can't you foresee how such a marriage would
turn out, have you no sense of decency?
If you force any girl to take a husband
against her will, you're gambling with her
                                      virtue;
she may intend to lead a life of honour,
but that depends on who you've chosen for her,
and those whose wives are famously unfaithful
have often driven them to that condition.
And after all it's quite hard to be faithful
to certain husbands cast in a certain mould;
and anyone who gives a girl away
to a man she can't stand is answerable
before God for whatever she might do.
So think what danger your plan puts you in.

ORGON: Do I need her to teach me how to live?

DORINE:	If you've got any sense, you'll listen to me.
ORGON:	Let us not waste our time, dear, on this
	nonsense:
	I am your father and I know what's best.
	It's true, I had promised you to Valère;
	but he's been seen more than once playing
	cards,
	and I suspect he may be a freethinker;
	I haven't seen a lot of him in church.
DORINE:	Why should he go exactly when you do?
	He's not, like others, just there to be seen.
ORGON:	I don't need your opinion. I just know
	Heaven smiles on Tartuffe and that's an asset
	second to none. This marriage will fulfil
	your wildest dreams, a series of sweet
	pleasures.
	You'll live together, faithfully in love,
	like two true children, like two turtle-doves.
	You'll never quarrel, and you'll find that you
	can turn him into anything you please.
DORINE:	A cuckold, for example, which is all
	she'll want to turn him into.
ORGON:	That's enough!
DORINE:	It's written all over him, it's in his stars;
	not all your daughter's virtue could resist it.
ORGON:	Will you stop interrupting me? Shut up,
	keep your nose out of other people's business.
DORINE:	I'm only trying to help.
	(*From now on, she interrupts him every time he turns away to speak to his daughter.*)
ORGON:	Well, don't; be quiet.
DORINE:	It's only because we love you . . .
ORGON:	I don't want
	to be loved.
DORINE:	Even so, I want to love you.
ORGON:	Ah!
DORINE:	See, your reputation is important

	to me, I hate to see you lay yourself
	open to general ridicule.
ORGON:	Shut up!
DORINE:	How could I let you contract such a marriage,
	in all conscience?
ORGON:	Will you be quiet, snake,
	before I . . .
DORINE:	I thought you were supposed to be
	religious.
ORGON:	So I am, but all this jabber
	is making my blood boil and I insist
	you hold your tongue.
DORINE:	Certainly. I won't say
	another word. But you can't stop me thinking.
ORGON:	Think all you like; just concentrate on not
	speaking to me, or . . . Enough.
	(*He turns to his daughter.*)
	In my wisdom,
	after mature consideration . . .
DORINE:	(*Aside*)
	It's
	infuriating not to be allowed
	to speak.
	(*She stops talking, as soon as he turns to her.*)
ORGON:	While not exactly very pretty,
	Tartuffe is . . .
DORINE:	(*Aside*)
	Off the side of Notre Dame!
ORGON:	Even if you could find no sympathy
	for all his gifts . . .
DORINE:	(*Aside*)
	This *is* your lucky day!
	(ORGON *turns to face* DORINE*; he watches her,*
	listening, with his arms folded.)
	If I was in her place, I'm telling you,
	no man would marry me against my will;
	or soon after the wedding he'd find out

	there's one way women can revenge
	themselves.
ORGON:	(*To* DORINE)
	I see, you're just ignoring what I said.
DORINE:	What's the matter? I'm not speaking to you.
ORGON:	What are you doing?
DORINE:	Talking to myself.
ORGON:	I see. (*Aside.*) I've never heard such insolence,
	she deserves a good smack and here it comes.
	(*He gets in a position to slap her; every time he glances at her,* DORINE *is standing up straight, in silence.*)
	My dear, you must agree to my suggestion . . .
	The husband I have . . . chosen for you is . . .
	(*To* DORINE)
	Well, speak up!
DORINE:	I have nothing else to say.
ORGON:	Surely there's something?
DORINE:	No, don't feel like it.
ORGON:	But I've been waiting.
DORINE:	You think I'm a fool?
ORGON:	Well, anyway, I insist on your obedience
	and your complete acceptance of my choice.
DORINE:	(*Running for it*)
	I wouldn't be seen dead with such a husband.
	(*He tries to slap her and misses.*)
ORGON:	That girl's a pest, I can't put up with her
	without surrendering to sinful rage.
	I really can't go on with our discussion;
	her insolence has goaded me to frenzy,
	I need some air to calm me down a bit.

DORINE, MARIANE.

DORINE: Well, have you lost your tongue, am I supposed
to play your part in this? How can you let
someone propose this idiotic plan,
without saying a single word against it?

MARIANE: What could I say? A father's power is absolute.

DORINE: Anything to stave off a threat like this.

MARIANE: What?

DORINE: Tell him you can't love at second hand.
Tell him you're marrying for your sake, not his.
Since you're the centre of attention here,
it's you, not him, your husband must appeal to;
and if he thinks Tartuffe is so attractive,
he's quite welcome to marry him himself.

MARIANE: I've never had the strength to raise a protest
against father's authority, I admit.

DORINE: Just a minute. Valère has made his move:
tell me, do you love him or do you not?

MARIANE: How can you be so unfair to my love,
Dorine? How can you ask me such a question?
Haven't I always confided in you,
and told you fifty times how much I love him?

DORINE: How do I know if all of that was true,
and whether you feel genuinely about him?

MARIANE: Dorine, it's very wrong of you to doubt it,
you know I've never hidden my true feelings.

DORINE: So then, you love him?

MARIANE: Yes, passionately.

DORINE: By all appearances, he loves you too?

MARIANE: I think he does.

DORINE: And both of you are most

	impatient to get married?
MARIANE:	Yes, we are.
DORINE:	So what d'you plan to do about this business?
MARIANE:	If they force me, I'm going to kill myself.
DORINE:	That's wonderful. I hadn't thought of that;
	'course, if you die, you'll avoid all these
	problems.
	What a brilliant way out! It makes me angry
	to have to listen to this kind of talk.
MARIANE:	There's no need to get in a huff, Dorine.
	You have no sympathy for people's suffering.
DORINE:	I have no sympathy for empty threats,
	or crumbling without putting up a fight.
MARIANE:	What d'you expect? I can't help being timid . . .
DORINE:	But perseverance should be part of love.
MARIANE:	And I have persevered: I love Valère.
	Isn't it up to him to win my hand
	from father?
DORINE:	What, when father is this clown,
	who's utterly besotted with Tartuffe,
	and breaks his firm agreement on the marriage,
	you think the blame should be put on Valère?
MARIANE:	Would it be right to show, by flat refusal
	or wild defiance, how much I'm in love?
	However fine he is, should I abandon
	my sex's modesty, my daughter's duty?
	Do you think I should publicize my love . . . ?
DORINE:	No, no, I wouldn't want that. Now I see,
	you want to marry Tartuffe after all,
	and now I stop to think, I was quite wrong
	to try to dissuade you. What right had I
	to quarrel with your wishes? He's a most
	eligible match is that Monsieur Tartuffe.
	Oh, no, he's nothing to be sneezed at, is he?
	I mean, you can't deny Monsieur Tartuffe's
	a man who knows his backside from his elbow.
	To be his better half, that's no small honour.

He's generally admired, he's of good birth,
at least he says he is, sort of well-built,
those red ears and that nice florid face:
the only danger is you'll be too happy.

MARIANE: Oh, God! . . .

DORINE: Can you imagine the elation?
To be the wife of such a handsome man!

MARIANE: Oh, stop it, please, and find some way to help.
I give up now, I'll do whatever you say.

DORINE: No, no, a daughter must obey her father,
even if he wants to marry her to an ape.
You're very lucky, why are you complaining?
You'll take the coach back to his little town,
and you'll meet all his uncles and his cousins,
you're certain to enjoy their conversation.
You'll be taken to all the best addresses
and welcomed there by all the dignitaries,
the bailiff's wife, the wife of the JP,
they'll get out their spare canvas chair for you.
Then there's the village fête to look forward to,
there'll be a ball, with a great orchestra,
consisting of a pair of bagpipers,
and, as a special treat, an organ-grinder,
and those amusing Punch and Judy shows.
And if your husband . . .

MARIANE: Do you want to kill
me?
Better if you could find some way to help.

DORINE: You mustn't ask me that.

MARIANE: Oh, please,
Dorine . . .

DORINE: No, it must go ahead now, you deserve it.

MARIANE: Dorine.

DORINE: No.

MARIANE: What I've told you . . .

DORINE: Nothing
doing.

Tartuffe's your man, you won't escape him
now.

MARIANE: You know I've always told you everything;
now help me . . .

DORINE: No. You're going to be
tartuffed.

MARIANE: I see. Well, since you're unmoved by my fate,
you'd best abandon me to my despair:
and let it be my ready consolation;
I know there's one sure way out of my
troubles.

DORINE: All right, come back: I'll try not to be angry.
In spite of everything, I can't help feeling
sorry for you.

MARIANE: If I'm to undergo
this cruel martyrdom, you see, Dorine,
I know it's going to be the death of me.

DORINE: Don't worry: I'm sure there's some clever
way . . .
But here's Valère himself.

SCENE FOUR

VALÈRE, MARIANE, DORINE.

VALÈRE: I have just heard
the most extraordinary piece of news.

MARIANE: What's that?

VALÈRE: That you are marrying Tartuffe.

MARIANE: It's true my father wants me to.

VALÈRE: Your father . . .

MARIANE: Has changed his mind. He's just this minute
told me.

VALÈRE: What, seriously?

MARIANE: Yes, seriously; he seems

	determined I should marry him.
VALÈRE:	And what do you intend to do now?
MARIANE:	I don't know.
VALÈRE:	Well, there's an honest answer. You don't know?
MARIANE:	No.
VALÈRE:	No?
MARIANE:	What's your advice?
VALÈRE:	Oh, my advice is to accept.
MARIANE:	That's your advice?
VALÈRE:	It is.
MARIANE:	You mean it?
VALÈRE:	Certainly, I mean it, it's a handsome offer, well worth your attention.
MARIANE:	Well, then, I'd better follow your advice.
VALÈRE:	I don't think that will be too hard for you.
MARIANE:	No harder than it was for you to give it.
VALÈRE:	I did so in the hope of giving pleasure.
MARIANE:	Whereas I shall now follow it to please you. (DORINE *withdraws upstage*.)
DORINE:	Well, let's see how they can get out of this.
VALÈRE:	Is this what love is? Was it just deceit when you. . . ?
MARIANE:	I'd rather not discuss that, please. You said quite openly that I should marry the husband I've been offered: I'm announcing that I intend to do so, following your excellent advice.
VALÈRE:	You shouldn't use my stand as an excuse: you'd already decided, and you're grasping at this silly pretext to justify breaking your word.
MARIANE:	It's true, you put it very well.
VALÈRE:	I'm sure;

	you never really loved me.

MARIANE: You're entitled
to your opinion.

VALÈRE: Yes, I am entitled;
and I may manage to forestall your plan,
by taking my proposal somewhere else.

MARIANE: I wouldn't be surprised; you're so
                                     good-looking . . .

VALÈRE: God, let's leave my looks out of it, shall we?
They can't be that good, as you've just yourself
demonstrated. But there is somebody,
who feels kindly for me and, now I'm free,
won't be ashamed to remedy my loss.

MARIANE: Your loss seems far from great, I'm sure you'll
                                                have
no difficulty finding consolation.

VALÈRE: You may be confident I'll do my best.
Being abandoned puts us on our mettle;
we must make every effort to forget
the person who's responsible, and even
if we can't quite succeed, we must pretend to:
to show oneself in love with someone faithless
would be the most unpardonable weakness.

MARIANE: What an exalted, lofty sentiment.

VALÈRE: I don't think anyone could disapprove.
I suppose you think that I should keep my love
for you alive and burning endlessly,
watching you fall into someone else's arms,
without the right to find some new allegiance
for the heart you've rejected?

MARIANE: Not at all;
that sounds the best idea, I wish you'd done it
already.

VALÈRE: Is that what you wish?

MARIANE: It is.

VALÈRE: Right, I'm not staying here to be insulted,
I'll do you a good turn by leaving.

(He starts to go, but doesn't get very far.)

MARIANE: Fine.

VALÈRE: *(Coming back)*
You should at least remember that it's you
who's driving me to this extreme.

MARIANE: I will.

VALÈRE: And that this plan is only following your
example.

MARIANE: Following my example, yes.

VALÈRE: *(Leaving)*
Well, that's enough: I'm leaving, like you said.

MARIANE: I'm pleased to hear it.

VALÈRE: *(Coming back again)*
This time it's for good.

MARIANE: Wonderful!
*(VALÈRE sets off again; when he reaches the door, he
turns back.)*

VALÈRE: What?

MARIANE: You what?

VALÈRE: Did you say
something?

MARIANE: Me? You're imagining things.

VALÈRE: Right then, I'm
off.
Goodbye.
(He moves slowly off.)

MARIANE: Goodbye.

DORINE: *(To MARIANE)*
Have you gone off your
head?
I've left you this long just to see how far
you'd go. Hey, Monsieur Valère!
*(She takes hold of his arm. VALÈRE pretends to
struggle furiously.)*

VALÈRE: What d'you
want,
Dorine?

38

DORINE:	Come here.
VALÈRE:	No, no, I'm too upset.
	It's what she wanted, so don't try and talk me out of it.
DORINE:	Stop it.
VALÈRE:	No, look, it's all settled.
DORINE:	Ah!
MARIANE:	(*Aside*)
	He can't bear the sight of me, he's only leaving because I'm here, I'd better go instead.
	(DORINE *leaves* VALÈRE *and runs after* MARIANE.)
DORINE:	Oh, now it's her! Where are you off to?
MARIANE:	Let go.
DORINE:	Come back.
MARIANE:	No, Dorine, it's no good.
VALÈRE:	(*Aside*)
	I see my presence is a torment to her, the best course is to free her of it now.
	(DORINE *leaves* MARIANE *and runs after* VALÈRE.)
DORINE:	What, again? No, damned if I'm going to let you!
	Stop this nonsense and come here, both of you.
	(*She tugs at them both.*)
VALÈRE:	(*To* DORINE)
	What do you want?
MARIANE:	(*To* DORINE)
	What are you trying to do?
DORINE:	Bring you together and get you out of this.
	(*To* VALÈRE)
	Have you gone mad to start this kind of row?
VALÈRE:	Didn't you hear the way she spoke to me?
DORINE:	(*To* MARIANE)
	And you, have you gone mad, losing your temper?
MARIANE:	Didn't you see the way he treated me?
DORINE:	(*To* VALÈRE)

	You're both as stupid as each other. All
	she wants is to be yours, I know that's true.
	(*To* MARIANE)
	He loves no one but you, all he wants is
	to marry you: I'll stake my life on it.
MARIANE:	(*To* VALÈRE)
	Well, then, why did you give me that advice?
VALÈRE:	Why did you ask me for it, I'd like to know?
DORINE:	You are both mad. Here, each give me a hand.
	(*To* VALÈRE)
	Come on.
	(VALÈRE *gives* DORINE *his hand.*)
VALÈRE:	My hand, what for?
DORINE:	(*To* MARIANE)
	And you as well.
	(MARIANE *also gives* DORINE *her hand.*)
MARIANE:	What use will that be?
DORINE:	My God, come here,
	quick.
	You love each other far more than you think.
	(VALÈRE *and* MARIANE *hold hands for a while without looking at each other. Then* VALÈRE *turns to* MARIANE.)
VALÈRE:	Don't be so grudging, give us a friendly look.
	(MARIANE *turns to* VALÈRE *and gives a little smile.*)
DORINE:	Of course, it's well known lovers are quite mad.
VALÈRE:	(*To* MARIANE)
	Don't you think I have some grounds for
	complaint?
	You must admit, it wasn't very nice
	to take such pleasure in upsetting me.
MARIANE:	Aren't you the most ungrateful man alive. . . ?
DORINE:	Can we leave this discussion for the moment
	and concentrate on fending off this wedding?
MARIANE:	Tell us what we should do.
DORINE:	Try everything.
	Your father can't be serious with this nonsense.
	All the same, you should react to his ravings

by giving an impression of consent,
so that in an emergency it'd be
easier for you to spin out the engagement.
The key thing in all this is playing for time.
You can develop sudden illnesses
to cause delay, or come across bad omens:
an argument with someone who's then died,
a broken mirror, dreams of muddy water.
The main thing is that they can't marry you
to him, or anyone, till you say, 'I do.'
Also, I'd say, to be on the safe side,
it's an idea not to be seen together.
(*To* VALÈRE)
So don't waste time, and get your friends to start
pressuring him to keep his promise to you.
(*To* MARIANE)
We must get your stepmother on our side
and ask her brother to keep trying. 'Bye.

VALÈRE: (*To* MARIANE)
To tell the truth, whatever we may try,
it's you I'm counting on.

MARIANE: (*To* VALÈRE)
                         Well, I can't answer
for what my father wants, but I know I'll
never belong to anyone but you.

VALÈRE: That's a great comfort! So whatever they . . .

DORINE: Lovers can't get enough of all this blather.
Now, will you go . . .
(VALÈRE *takes a step and then turns back.*)

VALÈRE: Just one thing . . .

DORINE: No
                                          more chat!
(*She pushes them both by the shoulder.*)
Now, you go this way, and you, you go that.

ACT THREE

SCENE ONE

DAMIS, DORINE.

DAMIS: I deserve to be struck dead on the spot
and treated like a miserable nothing
if I don't think up some brilliant idea,
and when I do no power on earth will stop me!

DORINE: Oh, please, there's no need to exaggerate;
it's only a suggestion of your father's.
Not every resolution's carried out,
there's many a slip.

DAMIS: I must scotch this swine's
plots,
there's two words I must whisper in his ear.

DORINE: Now, take it easy! Let your stepmother
deal with him as she's dealing with your father.
She has some kind of influence on Tartuffe;
she can say what she likes and he's always
indulgent, perhaps he's even smitten with her.
I hope to God he is! That would be fun.
In fact, she's summoned him on your behalf;
she wants to sound him out about this marriage
that's worrying you so much, she wants to know
the way he feels about it, and explain
to him the difficulties it would cause
if he was to encourage this idea.
His servant says I can't see him, he's praying;
but he also told me he'd be down soon.
So please go now and let me wait for him.

DAMIS: Why shouldn't I just be here while they're
talking?

DORINE: No. They must be alone.

DAMIS: I wouldn't say

	a word to him.
DORINE:	You're joking: we all know what a short fuse you're on, that's just the way to ruin everything. Now off you go.
DAMIS:	No, I can watch without losing my temper.
DORINE:	You're so annoying! Go on, here he comes.

SCENE TWO

TARTUFFE, LAURENT, DORINE.

TARTUFFE:	(*Noticing* DORINE) My hair shirt, Laurent, please put it away next to my birch, and I want you to pray for Heaven's eternal guidance. If there are visitors, tell them I'll be at the prison, distributing what few small coins I have.
DORINE:	(*Aside*) Posturing humbug!
TARTUFFE:	Yes, what do you want?
DORINE:	To tell you . . . (TARTUFFE *pulls a handkerchief out of his pocket.*)
TARTUFFE:	Oh, my goodness, just a moment, before you say another word, take this.
DORINE:	What for?
TARTUFFE:	Cover your breasts, I shouldn't have to be exposed to them, that kind of thing does damage to the soul and can give rise to guilty thoughts.
DORINE:	You're very vulnerable to temptation, I didn't know that flesh made such a big impression on your senses. I can't see why you should get overheated;

44

	I mean, I'm not so easy to arouse:
	for instance, I could look at you stark-naked,
	and not be tempted by a single inch.
TARTUFFE:	If you don't show a little modesty,
	I'll be obliged to leave you.
DORINE:	No, you won't,
	it's me who's going, so you can calm down;
	the only thing I have to say is this:
	Madame is on her way, she'd like a word.
TARTUFFE:	By all means!
DORINE:	(*Aside*)
	Ah, that's cheered him up! I
	think
	I must be right.
TARTUFFE:	Will she be long?
DORINE:	I think
	that's her now, yes, it is, I'll leave you to it.

SCENE THREE

ELMIRE, TARTUFFE.

TARTUFFE:	May God in all His infinite goodness grant you
	perpetual health in body and in soul,
	and bless you: that's His humblest suppliant's
	prayer!
ELMIRE:	I'm very grateful for your pious wishes.
	Sit down, let's make ourselves more
	comfortable.
TARTUFFE:	(*Sitting down*)
	I hope you've quite recovered from your illness.
ELMIRE:	(*Sitting down*)
	Oh, yes, thank you, the fever didn't last.
TARTUFFE:	My prayers are scarcely worthy of attracting
	grace from on high; but I must say their sole

45

	object has been your speedy convalescence.
ELMIRE:	I really think you show too much desire for my welfare.
TARTUFFE:	Your health is very precious; to bring it back I'd sacrifice my own.
ELMIRE:	That's taking Christian charity to its limits; I do appreciate your kindness, really.
TARTUFFE:	I do far less for you than you deserve.
ELMIRE:	I've been wanting to talk to you in private, I'm glad that we're alone together here.
TARTUFFE:	Yes, I'm delighted, it is such a pleasure to be alone with you for the first time: an opportunity I've often prayed for.
ELMIRE:	I thought we could just have a conversation in which you'd feel you might confide in me. (*Without showing himself,* DAMIS *half-opens the door of the closet, in which he's been hiding, in order to listen to the conversation.*)
TARTUFFE:	And I want nothing better than the chance, the privilege of baring my soul to you, and of assuring you that the protests I made against your visitors were nothing personal, they were prompted by my zeal and by an impulse to . . .
ELMIRE:	So I assumed, I know my welfare was your main concern. (TARTUFFE *squeezes the ends of her fingers.*)
TARTUFFE:	Of course it was, and such was my desire . . .
ELMIRE:	Ow, that hurts!
TARTUFFE:	It's just over-eagerness. I never meant to hurt you, I'd much rather . . . (*He puts his hand on her knee.*)
ELMIRE:	What are you doing?
TARTUFFE:	Just feeling your dress. Isn't it velvety?
ELMIRE:	Oh, no, please, don't. I'm very ticklish.

(*She moves her chair back, and* TARTUFFE *moves his chair closer. He starts feeling the lace on* ELMIRE's *bodice.*)

TARTUFFE: What workmanship!
It's wonderful the things they do these days.
My word, I've never seen anything like it.

ELMIRE: I'm sure. But can we get back to the point?
I've heard my husband wants to break his
           promise
and give his daughter to you. Is that true?

TARTUFFE: He said something about it; but, quite frankly,
that's not the happiness I'm pining for;
all my desires are concentrated on
a different set of wonderful attractions.

ELMIRE: You mean you have no time for earthly
           matters.

TARTUFFE: My heart is not entirely made of stone.

ELMIRE: I know your aspirations are toward Heaven,
that down here nothing can distract your will.

TARTUFFE: The love we feel for the eternal beauties
doesn't preclude a love for what is temporal,
and our senses can easily succumb
under the spell of God's perfect creations.
His glories are reflected in your sex,
but in your case it's more than that, He's
           revealed
His rarest wonders and lavished such beauties
on you, we're dazzled, we're carried away;
and I can't look at you, you perfect creature,
without admiring the Almighty in you,
struck to the heart with blazing love in front of
God's loveliest self-portrait. Oh, at first,
I was afraid this secret passion was
a cunning subterfuge of the Prince of Darkness;
and I even determined to avoid you,
thinking you might jeopardize my salvation.
But finally I realized, my sweet beauty:

in such a feeling there could be no guilt,
it could be reconciled with purity,
and that's when I surrendered myself to it.
I confess, it is very bold of me
to dare to offer you my love like this;
but I'm relying wholly on your kindness,
rather than on my own unworthiness.
My hopes, my well-being, my peace of mind
are in your hands, my suffering or my bliss
depend on you, and only you can make me
happy or unhappy, just as you choose.

ELMIRE: Well, that's a very gallant declaration,
if, to be honest, somewhat unexpected.
It seems to me you ought to have reflected
a little and held back from such a step.
A man whose reputation as a saint . . .

TARTUFFE: Why should a saint be any the less human?
Confronted with your heavenly attractions,
a man just gives way, how can he reflect?
It may seem strange for me to say such things;
but after all, Madame, I'm not an angel,
and if my declaration is blameworthy,
the real culprit is your enchanting beauty.
Ever since I first saw its superhuman,
radiant glory, you have ruled my heart.
The indescribable tenderness of your
divine expression broke down my resistance,
overcame all my fasting, prayers and weeping
and concentrated all my hopes on you.
I'm only voicing what you must have guessed
when I so often looked at you and sighed.
If you could bring yourself to show some favour
to your unworthy servant's tribulations,
if you would deign to stoop down to my level
and out of kindness offer me relief,
delicious prodigy, I guarantee
my eternal, unparalleled devotion.

Your reputation would be safe with me,
you'd run no risk of notoriety.
These libertines the ladies so admire
at court are ostentatious and loud-mouthed,
always bragging of conquests, of whose favours
no detail is too intimate to reveal;
their indiscretions and abuse of trust
degrade the very object of their worship.
People like us know how to love discreetly,
and how to keep it permanently secret.
Our own concern for our good character
acts as a guarantee for those we love,
and once you've given way, you'll find we offer
love without scandal, pleasure without fear.

ELMIRE: I've heard you out now, and your eloquence
is unambiguous enough, I think.
But aren't you worried that I might decide
to tell my husband about this proposal?
And that if he were told about your hopes
it might do damage to his friendship for you?

TARTUFFE: I know that you're too generous for that,
and that you will forgive my recklessness;
the violence of a passion which offends you
you will exonerate as human weakness,
and, bearing in mind your looks, you will
                                       acknowledge
that I'm not blind and men are flesh and blood.

ELMIRE: Others might take another line perhaps,
but I prefer to exercise discretion.
I shall say nothing of this to my husband;
but in return I'd like something from you:
I want you to support quite openly,
without beating about the bush, Valère's
marriage to Mariane, and to give up
your unfair influence and your desire
to enrich yourself with someone else's money,
and . . .

ELMIRE, DAMIS, TARTUFFE.
DAMIS *emerges from the closet in which he's been hiding.*

DAMIS: No, no, everyone must know about this.
I was in there and I heard everything;
it's as if Heaven led me there to crush
the hubris of a treacherous enemy,
and give me the potential for revenge
against his insolent hypocrisy,
the means to disabuse my father and
expose this monster's attempt to seduce you.

ELMIRE: No, Damis, it's enough he should improve
and try to be worthy of my reprieve.
I've given my promise, please don't make me
                                break it.
It isn't in my nature to make trouble;
a woman laughs off foolishness like this
and wouldn't dream of worrying her husband.

DAMIS: You have your reasons for that attitude
and I have mine for disagreeing with it.
I think to let him off would be a joke;
his insolence and sanctimoniousness
have got the better of my justified
protests too often and have caused too many
upheavals in this house. This liar has led
my father by the nose for far too long,
and done his best to undermine my love
as well as Valère's. Now Heaven has offered
an easy way of unmasking the traitor,
I have to take the opportunity,
it's far too providential to be missed;
to have it in my hand and let it go

would mean I would deserve to lose this
                                    chance.
ELMIRE: Damis . . .
DAMIS: No, please, I have to trust my
                                    judgement.
I couldn't be happier, and you won't persuade
                                    me
to forgo all the pleasures of revenge.
I have what I need to conclude this business;
and here's the man who'll put my mind at rest.

SCENE FIVE

ORGON, DAMIS, TARTUFFE, ELMIRE.

DAMIS: Now, listen, father, this should cheer you up,
               something's just happened which may startle
                                    you.
               It's a reward for all your kindnesses,
               acknowledged by this man with a fat payment.
               He's just been showing his great love for you,
               which doesn't even draw the line at making
               a cuckold of you; I've just caught him here
               making a proposition to your wife.
               You know her gentleness and her discretion;
               she wanted very much to keep it secret,
               but I just can't indulge his shamelessness:
               I think it would be quite wrong not to tell you.
ELMIRE: It's true, I don't think one should ever ruin
               a husband's peace of mind for trivial reasons;
               honour is not affected, it's enough
               for us to know how to defend ourselves.
               That's how I feel; and if I'd had the slightest
               influence on you, you would have kept quiet.

51

ORGON, DAMIS, TARTUFFE.

ORGON: My God, can it be possible, what they say?

TARTUFFE: Yes, brother, I am evil, I am guilty,
a wicked sinner sunk in iniquity,
the greatest criminal that ever lived.
Each second of my life is stained with filth,
it's one huge seething rubbish heap of vice,
and Heaven's clearly seized upon this chance
to humiliate me as a punishment.
I wouldn't have the arrogance to deny
whatever sin it is that I'm accused of.
So fuel your anger, believe what they say,
and throw me on the street like some
                            delinquent.
However great the shame you pile upon me,
it couldn't be as much as I deserve.

ORGON: (*To* DAMIS)
You wretch, how dare you fabricate this lie
and try to blot his purity and virtue?

DAMIS: You mean this hypocritical surrender
could make you doubt. . . ?

ORGON: Be quiet, you little
                                  pest!

TARTUFFE: No, let him speak; it's wrong of you to blame
                                    him,
you'd do better to believe what he says.
Why should you favour me in this dispute?
After all, how do you know what I might
be capable of? Do you trust mere show?
You think I'm better just because I seem so?
No, no, you're letting yourself be tricked by

appearances and, I'm sorry to say,
I'm not at all the man I'm thought to be.
Everyone takes me for a good man, but
the simple truth is I'm entirely worthless.
(*He turns to* DAMIS.)
Come on, my boy, speak up: call me a traitor,
a lost soul, a degenerate, a thief,
a murderer; crush me with viler names;
I won't deny them, I've deserved them all,
and on my knees I welcome this disgrace
in expiation of my life of crime.

ORGON: (*To* TARTUFFE)
You go too far.
(*To* DAMIS)
             Aren't you ashamed, you
                        wretch?

DAMIS: You mean you're taken in by this . . . ?

ORGON: Be quiet,
you gallows-bird!
(*To* TARTUFFE)
             Oh, please, brother, get up!
(*To* DAMIS)
Scum!

DAMIS: Maybe . . .

ORGON: Shut up!

DAMIS: This is too much,
                       I . . .

ORGON: If you say one more word, I'll break your arms.

TARTUFFE: For God's sake, brother, please don't lose your
                        temper.
I'd rather suffer any punishment
than see him take a scratch on my account.

ORGON: (*To* DAMIS)
You upstart!

TARTUFFE: Leave him be. If necessary,
I'll ask you to forgive him on my knees . . .

ORGON: (*To* TARTUFFE)

You can't be serious!
(*To* DAMIS)
                              See how kind he is,
you louse!

DAMIS: But . . .
ORGON: Silence!
DAMIS: What? I . . .
ORGON: I said,
                                          silence!

I know your motives for attacking him:
all of you hate him and I've had to watch
my wife, my children and my servants hound
                                          him.
No method is too brazen when it comes
to driving this good person from my house.
But the more you try to get rid of him,
the better ways I'll find to keep him here;
and to annihilate my family's arrogance,
I'm going to give my daughter to him, soon.

DAMIS: You're going to force her to accept his hand?
ORGON: Yes, wretch, and, to spite you, this very
                                          evening.
Ha, I defy you all, I'm going to teach you
that I'm in charge here and I'll be obeyed.
So take back what you said this minute, liar,
down on your knees and ask him to forgive you!

DAMIS: Who, me? Me ask this unscrupulous fake. . . ?
ORGON: So you refuse, you ruffian, and insult him?
A stick, bring me my stick!
(*To* TARTUFFE)
                              And you let go!
(*To* DAMIS)
Out of my house, and don't you dare come
                                          back!

DAMIS: All right, all right, I'm leaving . . .
ORGON: Get out,
                                          now!

I hereby disinherit you, you gaolbird;
the only thing I'll give you is my curse.

SCENE SEVEN

ORGON, TARTUFFE.

ORGON: What a way to insult a man of God!
TARTUFFE: Oh, Lord, forgive his trespasses against me!
           (*To* ORGON)
           Ah, if you only knew how much it hurts
           when people try to blacken me in your eyes . . .
ORGON: Don't!
TARTUFFE: Just to think of the ingratitude
           is such a cruel torment to my soul . . .
           The horror of it . . . My heart is so heavy,
           I can't speak, this will be the death of me.
           (ORGON *bursts into tears, and runs to the door through
           which he has driven* DAMIS.)
ORGON: You louse! I'm sorry I restrained myself,
           I should have knocked you senseless there and
                                                    then.
           Calm down, now, brother, don't get so upset.
TARTUFFE: It's time we put an end to these dissensions.
           I know I've been a cause of trouble here,
           I can see no alternative to my leaving.
ORGON: You can't be serious!
TARTUFFE: They hate me here,
           they're trying to make you doubt my integrity.
ORGON: So what? You think I'm going to listen to
                                                    them?
TARTUFFE: They won't give up attacking, that's for sure,
           and accusations which you now reject
           are bound to take their toll eventually.
ORGON: Impossible.

TARTUFFE:	Brother, you know a wife can easily delude her husband.
ORGON:	No, never.
TARTUFFE:	If I were to leave here forthwith, they'd have no grounds for these attacks; so let me.
ORGON:	No, you must stay, my life depends on it.
TARTUFFE:	Well, in that case, I'll have to sacrifice myself. And yet . . .
ORGON:	What?
TARTUFFE:	No, we'll say no more. I know what's necessary. Honour is a fragile plant and our friendship obliges me to prevent this rumour and suspicion by avoiding your wife. I won't be seen . . .
ORGON:	No, I defy them all, you'll spend time with her, my greatest pleasure is to make them angry, I want you to be seen with her constantly. And that's not all: to show them what I think, I'll make you my sole heir and waste no time in handing over all my worldly goods. You're my friend, you will be my son-in-law, dearer to me by far than my own son, my wife or my relations. Won't you please accept my offer?
TARTUFFE:	Well, God's will be done!
ORGON:	Poor boy! Come on, let's go and draft the papers, and let that jealous lot gag on their own spite!

ACT FOUR

CLÉANTE, TARTUFFE.

CLÉANTE: Yes, everyone's discussing it, believe
me, and the verdict's not to your advantage;
I'm pleased to have this opportunity
to give you my opinion in a few words.
I don't propose to get into the details;
forget all that and let's assume the worst.
Suppose Damis has behaved badly and
falsely accused you, would it not be Christian
to overlook the sin and to suppress
any desire for vengeance? Ought you to
allow a son to be driven out of
his father's house because of a dispute
with you? I tell you frankly, I repeat,
people of every class are shocked by this.
If you take my advice, you'll make peace here
and not let matters be pushed to extremes.
Forget your anger, offer it up to God
and reconcile a father with his son.

TARTUFFE: As far as I'm concerned, I would like nothing
better, I have no animus against him.
I forgive him, I don't blame him at all,
I would do anything I could for him;
but from God's point of view, it's just not on,
and if he comes back, I shall have to leave.
After his unprecedented behaviour,
any contact between us would invite
scandal: God knows what might not be
                            inferred!
I'd be accused of pure expedience,
and everyone would say that, out of guilt,

I was pretending to forgive my enemy,
that I was afraid of him and hoped I could
in some clandestine way pay for his silence.

CLÉANTE: These are just so many specious excuses.
Your reasoning is far too tortuous.
Why should you fret about God's point of view?
Does He need your help to chastise the guilty?
Leave it to Him to wreak His own revenges;
He tells us to forgive sinners, remember,
and not to take account of human judgements
when following His sovereign commands.
This weak concern for what people might think
surely can't be allowed to override
the majesty of doing good? No, no;
let's follow God's commandments every time,
and not confuse ourselves with other concepts.

TARTUFFE: I've already explained that I forgive him,
and therefore I am following God's
                           commandments;
but after this scandal and today's insults,
there's no commandment says I have to live
                            with him.

CLÉANTE: And is there a commandment says you should
acquiesce in this mad whim of his father's,
and accept his gift to you of a fortune
on which justice must tell you you've no claim?

TARTUFFE: Those who know me would never dream of
                           thinking
that this is a result of my self-seeking.
The riches of this world have very little
appeal to me, I'm not one to be dazzled
by their illusory glow; and if Orgon
wants me to have this gift and I decide
to take it, it will only be because
otherwise, to be honest, I'd be worried
in case all of that money were to fall
into the wrong hands; and end up with people

who'd use their share for evil purposes,
rather than keeping it, as I intend to,
for God's glory and the welfare of my
                                    neighbour.

CLÉANTE: Oh, spare yourself these dainty inhibitions,
which are offensive to the rightful heir.
Let him come into his inheritance
at his own risk, and don't distress yourself;
just think, better for him to squander it,
than for you to be charged with cheating him.
I'm only startled that you seem to be
quite unembarrassed by this proposition;
I mean, is there some old religious maxim
says thou shalt plunder the legitimate heir?
And if God really has implanted in you
this inability to live with Damis,
which can't be overcome, would it not be
better to show discretion and withdraw
than to allow this quite unreasonable
hounding out of a son on your account?
Now that would be a sign of character . . .

TARTUFFE: You must excuse me now, it's half-past three,
and I'm required upstairs to fulfil
certain religious duties, much as I hate
to leave you.

CLÉANTE: (*Alone*)
                            Ha!

SCENE TWO

ELMIRE, MARIANE, DORINE, CLÉANTE.

DORINE: (*To* CLÉANTE)
                    Please, sir, help us to help
                                            her:

she's in a dreadful state and this agreement
her father's fixed up for this evening has
driven her to despair. Look, here he comes:
let's try our best, by cunning or brute force,
to frustrate this abominable plan.

SCENE THREE

ORGON, ELMIRE, MARIANE, CLÉANTE, DORINE.

ORGON: Oh, good! I'm glad I've found you all together.
              (*To* MARIANE)
              Now here is something which should raise a
                                   smile:
              this contract—you must know what it's about.

MARIANE: (*On her knees*)
              God knows how painful this is, and for His
                                   sake,
              by anything that's capable of touching
              your heart, relax your father's rights a little,
              exempt my love from having to obey you.
              Don't impose this harsh law and so reduce me
              to wish to God that I were not your daughter;
              and please don't ruin my life for me, father,
              this life you gave me. If you must forbid me
              to belong to the man I love and thwart
              the hopes that I have been allowed to cherish,
               at least, I beg you on my knees, be kind
              and don't condemn me to belong to a man
              I loathe: don't exercise your power on me
              and drive me to do something desperate.

ORGON: (*Feeling himself weaken*)
              Now, come on, steel yourself, no human
                                weakness!

MARIANE: I have nothing against your feeling for him,

60

	display it all you like, give him your money,
	and if that's not enough, add mine as well.
	I'd agree happily, it's yours, but can't you
	just draw the line at offering him my body?
	Let me use up my sad remaining days
	in the austere enclosure of a convent.
ORGON:	I see, you're one of those who turns religious
	at the first setback to your amorous plans!
	On your feet! The more repulsive you find him,
	the more improving it will be for you.
	Use this marriage to mortify your senses,
	now that's all, I don't want any more nagging.
DORINE:	But what. . . ?
ORGON:	And you shut up, mind your own business:
	don't you dare speak, I utterly forbid it.
CLÉANTE:	If you'd allow just one word of advice . . .
ORGON:	Yes, your advice is always admirable,
	well argued, and I do value it greatly;
	but you won't mind if this time I ignore it.
ELMIRE:	(*To* ORGON)
	I don't know what to say about all this,
	I'm staggered by your blindness. You must be
	infatuated and obsessed with him,
	to overlook what's happened here today.
ORGON:	Seeing's believing, with all due respect.
	I know how indulgent you are towards my son,
	and that you were afraid to contradict him,
	when he tried playing that trick on the poor boy.
	You were too calm to be believable,
	you would have looked a good deal more upset.
ELMIRE:	Need we react quite so ferociously
	when someone just declares his love for us?
	Are blazing eyes and spitting out insults
	the only possible response to it?
	My way is just to laugh at these approaches,

I get no pleasure out of melodrama.
I think we should be calm and sensible,
and I've no time for those rampaging prudes
whose virtue's red in tooth and claw, and who
would scratch your eyes out at the first excuse;
Heaven preserve us from such saintliness!
I'm for integrity without shrewishness,
I think a chilly and discreet refusal
is as effective a rebuff as any.

ORGON: I know my mind and I'm not changing it.

ELMIRE: Again, I'm staggered by this curious weakness.
But how would it affect your unbelief,
if I could show you we were telling the truth?

ORGON: Show me?

ELMIRE: Yes.

ORGON: Rubbish!

ELMIRE: Suppose I found a
                                  way
to prove it beyond any doubt?

ORGON: Absurd!

ELMIRE: What a man! Won't you answer me at least?
I don't ask you to take our word for it;
suppose we found a place somewhere round
                            here,
where you could see and hear quite clearly,
                           then
what would you have to say about this good
                           man?

ORGON: In that case, I'd say . . . no, no, I'd say
                         nothing,
because it couldn't happen.

ELMIRE: This delusion
has lasted far too long, and I am tired
of being accused of lying. It's high time
I gave myself the satisfaction of
showing you everything we've said is true.

ORGON: All right, I'll take you at your word. Let's see

	you keep your promise.
ELMIRE:	(*To* DORINE)
	Bring him here to me.
DORINE:	(*To* ELMIRE)
	He's cunning and he may not be so easy
	to catch out.
ELMIRE:	No; in love, deceit is easy,
	vanity leads people to fool themselves.
	Bring him downstairs.
	(*She turns to* CLÉANTE *and* MARIANE.)
	And you two'd better
	go.

SCENE FOUR

ELMIRE, ORGON.

ELMIRE:	Let's move this table, you get underneath.
ORGON:	You what?
ELMIRE:	It's quite important you're well
	hidden.
ORGON:	But why under this table?
ELMIRE:	Oh, my God!
	Do what you're told, I have my plan, you'll see.
	Come on, get under it, and when you're there,
	keep quiet and make sure you can't be seen.
ORGON:	I must say, this is really very silly,
	but I can't wait to see you prove your point.
ELMIRE:	I don't believe you'll have any complaints.
	(*He's now under the table.*)
	You mustn't be surprised if I sound strange,
	or be at all shocked. Whatever I say,
	remember I have promised to convince you,
	and must be given free rein. I shall coax,
	since I'm reduced to this, this hypocrite

to take his mask off, and I shall encourage
his insolent desires and stimulate
his recklessness. Since all this is for you,
this pretence of responding to him with
the intention of fooling him, I'll only
stop it when you acknowledge you were wrong,
so things will go as far as you allow them.
It's up to you to interrupt his ardour,
when you consider they've gone far enough;
protect your wife and don't expose me to
any more than you need to be convinced.
It's your business and you're in charge and . . .
                                          Here
he comes; stay there and mind he doesn't see
                                              you.

SCENE FIVE

TARTUFFE, ELMIRE, ORGON, *hidden under the table.*

TARTUFFE: I'm told you asked to see me in this room.
ELMIRE: Yes, there's a secret I must tell you. But,
before I do, would you please close the door,
and make sure no one's likely to surprise us.
(TARTUFFE *goes to close the door and comes back.*)
We don't want a repeat of what just happened
for anything, I've never been so shocked.
Damis gave me a dreadful fright, on your
behalf, and, as you saw, I did my best
to calm him down and frustrate his intentions.
It's true I was so worried that it never
occurred to me to contradict his story;
but, thank God, for that very reason things
turned out much better and less dangerously.
Your reputation soon dispelled the storm,

my husband couldn't think badly of you;
and to show his contempt for crude suspicions,
he wants us to spend lots of time together;
and that's why I can be alone with you
here, without any fear of being judged,
and what allows me to reveal to you
what I should perhaps keep back a little longer:
that I'm prepared to entertain your suit.

TARTUFFE: I'm not quite sure I follow you, Madame,
just now you gave a very different answer.

ELMIRE: Oh, well, if my refusal put you off,
you must know very little about women!
You're no good at interpreting what's meant
by such an obviously weak defence.
On these occasions modesty is bound
to be in conflict with our tender feelings.
However right yielding to love may feel,
it's always slightly shaming to admit it.
At first we fight against it; but the way
we do so is a sign of our surrender;
our voice, for virtue's sake, protesting feebly
against our instincts, gives the kind of no
which promises you everything. Well, now,
I suppose that's a pretty damning confession,
I haven't paid much heed to modesty;
but, since it's in the open now at last,
would I have tried so hard to silence Damis?
I ask you, would I have so quietly listened
to that long declaration of your love?
Would I have taken it the way I did
unless something about it gave me pleasure?
And when I tried to blackmail you myself
not to accept this newly arranged wedding,
what did my urgency suggest to you,
if not that you now meant a lot to me,
and that this proposed marriage would upset

me,

	by, at the very least, making me share
	a love I wanted for myself alone?
TARTUFFE:	To hear such words from such a lovely mouth
	is exquisitely pleasurable, Madame;
	their honey sends unprecedented sweetness
	flowing in long draughts through my entire

system.

My main concern is to be fortunate
enough to please you and my greatest blessing
will be to fulfil your desires: but
forgive me if I take the liberty
of casting some small doubt on my good

fortune.

What you say might be a straightforward trick
to make me break off this impending marriage;
And, to be brutally honest, I shan't trust
these delicious suggestions you have made
until I get a taste of what I crave
to reassure me there's been no mistake
and instil in me lasting confidence
in just how generous you mean to be.
(ELMIRE *coughs to alert* ORGON.)

ELMIRE: Surely you don't have to move quite so fast
and exhaust all the possibilities
in one go? To make such an intimate
confession to you practically killed me:
and now I find it's not enough for you.
You mean you won't be satisfied until
this thing has gone as far as it can go?

TARTUFFE: An undeserving man can never quite
rely on hope. And conversation's not
a firm basis for love. It's all too easy
to have one's doubts about a glorious future:
once I've enjoyed it, then I'll believe in it.
You see, I don't think I deserve your kindness,
I can't accept my boldness has paid off,
I won't believe it, not until you find

	some realistic method to convince me.
ELMIRE:	My God, now you're behaving like a tyrant,
	and plunging me into a strange confusion!
	Your love has taken passionate control,
	and your desire's so violently demanding!
	Is there no way out? Won't you give a girl
	a breathing space? And is it right to make
	such mercilessly rigorous demands,
	and take advantage so insistently
	of this weakness you know I have for you?
TARTUFFE:	But why, if you approve of my advances,
	refuse me the definitive credential?
ELMIRE:	But how can I agree to what you want
	without, as you would say, offending God?
TARTUFFE:	If God is all you're worrying about,
	leave it to me to deal with that problem,
	you mustn't let that hold you back at all.
ELMIRE:	We're always told we must fear Heaven's
	judgements!
TARTUFFE:	I can dispel these ludicrous alarms,
	I know the art of freeing inhibitions.
	It's true that certain pleasures are forbidden
	by God; but there are ways of getting round
	this.
	Depending on one's needs, there is a method
	of loosening the fetters of one's conscience,
	setting the purity of our intentions
	against the evil of the deed itself.
	I'll explain these mysteries some other time;
	all you need do for now is what I tell you.
	Don't be afraid to fulfil my desires;
	I'll be responsible for everything
	and take the sin upon myself, Madame.
	(ELMIRE *coughs louder.*)
	That is a bad cough.
ELMIRE:	Yes, it's misery.
	(TARTUFFE *offers* ELMIRE *a twist of paper.*)

TARTUFFE:	Perhaps it would help to suck a piece of liquorice?
ELMIRE:	This cold has clung on, I can't seem to shift it, I don't think it would help much to suck anything.
TARTUFFE:	Well, that is trying.
ELMIRE:	Yes, unspeakably.
TARTUFFE:	Anyway, I can easily remove your scruples: this will be completely secret, I can assure you, and the only evil is to make a great noise about things. What constitutes the offence is public scandal. Sinning in silence is no sin at all. (*Another bout of coughing from* ELMIRE.)
ELMIRE:	All right, I see there's no alternative but to submit and give you what you want; clearly you can't be happy with a promise, and nothing less will do. I can't deny, I don't want to go this far and I do it against my better judgement; all the same, since you insist on making me and won't believe in my assurances and need more palpable corroboration, I must grit my teeth and try to keep you happy. And if agreeing to it is a crime, so much the worse for the man who's behind it, forcing me to it, it won't be my fault.
TARTUFFE:	Yes, you leave it to me, Madame, you'll find . . .
ELMIRE:	Just open that door, will you, and make sure my husband isn't in the gallery.
TARTUFFE:	Why worry about him? Between ourselves, he's very easy to manipulate. He takes a pride in our relationship, I've got him so that he wouldn't believe it even if he saw us . . .
ELMIRE:	Never mind, just go, and have a really good look round out there.

ORGON, ELMIRE.
ORGON *emerges from underneath the table.*

ORGON:	So you were right, what an appalling man!
	I can't get over it, it's such a shock.
ELMIRE:	What, already? There must be some mistake.
	Get back under the tablecloth, you're early;
	wait till he's finished, to be on the safe side,
	I don't think you should make unfair
	assumptions.
ORGON:	He's worse than any devil out of Hell.
ELMIRE:	Good God, now, don't go jumping to
	conclusions!
	Before you change your mind, I think you
	should
	be properly convinced, so don't be hasty,
	I wouldn't want you to make a mistake.
	(*She hides* ORGON *behind her.*)

TARTUFFE, ELMIRE, ORGON.

TARTUFFE:	(*Without seeing* ORGON)
	Nothing can stop me being happy now:
	I've checked all round, there's no one, my
	delight . . .
ORGON:	(*Stopping him*)
	Slow down! You're letting your desire run
	rampant,
	I wouldn't let yourself get too excited.

So, my good man, you thought you could
deceive me!

When you decide to give in to temptation,
no one could say you do the thing by halves!
Marrying my daughter, lusting for my wife!
I couldn't believe that it was really happening.
I kept waiting for you to change your tune;
but I think now we've had quite enough proof:
I'm satisfied in my mind, that's all I need.

ELMIRE: (*To* TARTUFFE)
I did all this against my better judgement;
I couldn't think of an alternative.

.TARTUFFE: You mean you think . . . ?

ORGON: Oh, please, let's have
no fuss.

Take yourself off without further ado.

TARTUFFE: I never meant . . .

ORGON: There's no point in all this;
Will you, this minute, get out of my house!

TARTUFFE: No, you get out, because it's my house now:
it won't do you the slightest good to grub up
these cheap excuses to get rid of me;
attacking me's more dangerous than you think,
I have a way of punishing impostors,
avenging this insult to God and making
people who try to throw me out repent.

SCENE EIGHT

ELMIRE, ORGON.

ELMIRE: What does he mean?

ORGON: My God, what shall I do?
This could be serious.

ELMIRE: Why?

70

ORGON:	What he just said:
	I fear tha˙ deed of gift was a mistake.
ELMIRE:	What deed of gift?
ORGON:	It's all signed, I'm afraid.
	But something else he said disturbed me more.
ELMIRE:	What?
ORGON:	I'll explain; but first of all, let's see
	if that attaché case is still upstairs.

ACT FIVE

ORGON, CLÉANTE.

CLÉANTE:	Where are you off to?
ORGON:	Oh, I wish I knew.
CLÉANTE:	It seems to me the first thing we must do
	is to discuss the possibilities.
ORGON:	My main worry is the attaché case;
	it's much more serious than all the rest.
CLÉANTE:	Is what's in this attaché case a secret?
ORGON:	Argas, that friend of mine who was in trouble,
	left it with me in strictest confidence.
	He sought me out before he fled abroad;
	from what he said, I gather it contains
	essential private and financial papers.
CLÉANTE:	Why did you hand it over to Tartuffe?
ORGON:	To ease my conscience. I went straight to him,
	that traitor, and confided in him; he
	persuaded me to give the case to him,
	on the grounds that, if anybody asked,
	I could deny I had it and still keep
	my conscience clear of any perjury.
CLÉANTE:	I'd say things looked black for you; and, to be frank,
	this indiscretion and the deed of gift
	were undertaken by you much too lightly.
	You've put yourself in pawn to him; and since
	he does have such great power over you,
	provoking him was desperately unwise,
	you ought to have tried harder to placate him.
ORGON:	Who could imagine that devout façade
	could hide such double-dealing wickedness?
	To think I took him in when he had nothing . . .

Well, he's the last religious man I'll trust;
in future I'll recoil from them in horror,
and never miss a chance to be their scourge.

CLÉANTE: Oh, not another of your tantrums, please!
You don't know what a happy medium is;
your reason never coincides with reason,
you always lurch from one excess to another.
You realize your mistake, that you were
                                        duped
by a false piety, but what's the point
of trying to make up for it by falling
into an even bigger trap and not
seeing the difference between men of honour
and this contemptible degenerate?
Just because one thief has, with his veneer
of hypocritical austerity,
brazenly cheated you, you then assume
everyone is like that and genuinely
religious people don't exist today!
Leave senseless thoughts like that to atheists;
learn to distinguish virtue and its semblance,
don't be too careless with your admiration,
and show a necessary moderation.
If possible, don't fall for hypocrites;
but, equally, don't attack true devotion,
and, if you can't help going to extremes,
better to make the same mistake again.

SCENE TWO

DAMIS, ORGON, CLÉANTE.

DAMIS: Is it true that this wretch is threatening you,
father, forgetting all your kindness to him,
and that with vile, infuriating pride,

74

	he's turned your generosity against you?
ORGON:	Yes, my son, and I've never suffered so much.
DAMIS:	Leave it to me, I'm going to cut his ears off.

There's no point holding back against that kind
of
shamelessness; yes, I'll get you out of this,
there's only one answer: I'll beat his head in.

CLÉANTE: The voice of youth. Now, will you please calm
down!
We're living in an age and in a kingdom
where violence is never a solution.

SCENE THREE

MADAME PERNELLE, MARIANE, ELMIRE, DORINE, DAMIS, ORGON,
CLÉANTE.

MME PERNELLE: What's happening? What are these dreadful
rumours?

ORGON: Unprecedented things, which I have witnessed,
the rewards of my generosity.
I take a poor man in most willingly;
I put him up and treat him like my brother;
I load him with new blessings every day;
I offer him my daughter and my money;
and all the while this criminal, this pig
nurtures a black plot to seduce my wife;
and not even content with that disgrace,
he dares to threaten me with my own gifts
and wants to use the weapons, with which my
foolish kindness has armed him, to destroy me,
to take the money I've transferred to him
and bring me down to what he was: a beggar.

DORINE: Poor boy!

MME PERNELLE: My dear, I really can't believe

	he could possibly do something so wicked.
ORGON:	What did you say?
MME PERNELLE:	People are always jealous of a really good man.
ORGON:	What can you mean?
MME PERNELLE:	This is a strange household and it's well known how much he's hated.
ORGON:	Hated? What's that to do with what I've just been saying?
MME PERNELLE:	When you were a little boy, I told you fifty times: in this world, virtue's always persecuted; the envious may die, but envy, never.
ORGON:	But what has this to do with what's just happened?
MME PERNELLE:	I expect they've made up all sorts of stories.
ORGON:	I've already explained, I saw it all.
MME PERNELLE:	There's nothing so ingenious as a gossip.
ORGON:	I'll swing for you yet, mother. Will you listen? I saw him do these wicked things myself.
MME PERNELLE:	There's always poison spread by idle tongues, no one on earth can get away from that.
ORGON:	This conversation is ridiculous. I saw him, understand, I saw him, saw him with my own eyes, what I did is described as seeing. How many more times must I repeat myself, must I shout myself hoarse?
MME PERNELLE:	Appearances deceive, often as not, you mustn't always go by what you see.
ORGON:	I'm going mad.
MME PERNELLE:	Suspicion's human nature, and good is often mistaken for evil.
ORGON:	I'm to suppose the urge to kiss my wife has some religious motive?
MME PERNELLE:	It's as well

	not to accuse people without just cause;
	You should have waited, to make really certain.
ORGON:	Good God, was there a way to be more certain?
	I should have waited till, in front of me,
	he . . . no, you'll make me say things I regret.
MME PERNELLE:	No, he's too pure, too much in love with virtue,
	I simply can't bring myself to believe
	he'd do the things that you accuse him of.
ORGON:	You're making me so angry, I just don't
	know what I would say, if you weren't my
	mother.
DORINE:	(*To* ORGON)
	That's how it goes, sir, and it serves you right:
	you wouldn't listen and neither will she.
CLÉANTE:	We're wasting time with all this nonsense,
	which
	we should be using to draw up some plans.
	We can't afford to dream, these are real
	threats.
DAMIS:	You really think he'd dare to see them through?
ELMIRE:	He wouldn't have the face to bring
	proceedings,
	he would seem just too blatantly ungrateful.
CLÉANTE:	(*To* ORGON)
	I wouldn't bank on it: he'll work out ways
	to justify his handiwork against you;
	and I've seen people caught in a labyrinth,
	once the religious clique is down on them,
	on much less evidence. And, as I said,
	knowing his power, you shouldn't have
	provoked him.
ORGON:	You're right; but how could I help it? How
	could I
	control my fury at his arrogance?
CLÉANTE:	I wish there was some way of building a
	negotiated settlement between you.
ELMIRE:	If I'd known he was so well armed against us,

I'd never have given him fresh ammunition,
I'm so . . .
(ORGON *sees* MONSIEUR LOYAL *approaching*.)

ORGON: (*To* DORINE)
           What does that man want? Go and
                       ask him.
A visitor just now is all I need!

SCENE FOUR

MONSIEUR LOYAL, MADAME PERNELLE, ORGON, DAMIS, MARIANE,
DORINE, ELMIRE, CLÉANTE.
M. LOYAL, *still upstage, speaks to* DORINE.

M. LOYAL: Good afternoon, dear sister. May I speak
to Monsieur Orgon?
DORINE: He has company.
I doubt he can see anyone right now.
M. LOYAL: I'm not here to make a nuisance of myself.
I don't think he'll have cause to regret my
visit; I'm here to do him a good turn.
DORINE: What name is it?
M. LOYAL: Just tell him that I'm here
for his own good, on Monsieur Tartuffe's
                          behalf.
DORINE: (*To* ORGON)
He's quite polite. He's here on Monsieur
                   Tartuffe's
behalf—he says he's doing you a favour.
CLÉANTE: (*To* ORGON)
You must see who he is and what he wants.
ORGON: Perhaps he's come to make a settlement.
How ought I to behave?
CLÉANTE: Don't show your
                     anger;

	and if he talks peace, you must listen to him.
M. LOYAL:	(*To* ORGON)
	How do you do, sir. God protect you from
	your enemies and grant you all I'd wish you!
ORGON:	(*Quietly to* CLÉANTE)
	That's a good start, it confirms my impression,
	I think it does imply a settlement.
M. LOYAL:	I've always been devoted to your family,
	I was once in your father's service.
ORGON:	Sir,
	I'm ashamed to admit, you must forgive me,
	I don't know who you are or what your name
	is.
M. LOYAL:	My name is Loyal, I'm from Normandy,
	I hold the much respected post of bailiff.
	For forty years I've been so fortunate,
	thank God, as to discharge my task with
	honour;
	and I am here, with your permission, sir,
	to serve you with this writ . . .
ORGON:	You mean
	you've come. . . ?
M. LOYAL:	Now, let's not have a scene, sir: all I have
	is this summons here, this eviction order,
	which says you must forthwith, without delay,
	remove yourself, your family, your effects . . .
ORGON:	What! Move out, me?
M. LOYAL:	Yes, sir, if you don't
	mind.
	As you're no doubt aware, there is no question
	that at the present moment this house here
	belongs to our revered Monsieur Tartuffe.
	From now on he is lord and master of
	your possessions, by virtue of a contract,
	legally drawn up, incontestable,
	which I happen to have about my person.
DAMIS:	(*To* M. LOYAL)

You've got a nerve.

M. LOYAL: I'm not obliged to deal
with you, sir; this is Monsieur Orgon's
business:
and he's a reasonable sort of chap,
who knows full well a man must do his duty ·
and wouldn't ever want to obstruct justice.

ORGON: But . . .

M. LOYAL: Yes, I know, sir, you would never
dream
of playing up, and, as an honest man,
you'll let me carry out my orders here.

DAMIS: You're heading the right way to feel my stick
laid right across your black gown, Monsieur
bailiff.

M. LOYAL: (*To* ORGON)
Tell your son to shut up or go away;
I'd hate to find it necessary to make
a reference to this in my report.

DORINE: (*Aside*)
Monsieur Loyal: he's not very well-named.

M. LOYAL: I always have been very well-disposed
towards men of good will; and that's the reason
I volunteered for this particular job,
to comfort you and help you out and make sure
they didn't send a man who, lacking my
personal sympathy for you, might have
approached the matter less respectfully.

ORGON: What's so respectful about turning people
out on the streets?

M. LOYAL: You'll have plenty of time.
I'll suspend execution of the writ
until tomorrow. Oh, there's just one thing:
I'll have to spend the night here with about
ten of my men. There'll be no noise, no trouble.
I will need, and before you go to bed, please,
it's only a formality, the keys.

I guarantee your sleep won't be disturbed,
and there'll be no unnecessary suffering.
You just be ready, first thing in the morning,
to clear out every last household utensil.
My men will help you, every one's hand-picked
to render you assistance with the move.
I don't think one can say fairer than that;
and as I've been so lenient with you,
I would request a corresponding temperance
on your part, as I go about my duties.

ORGON: (*Quietly*)
I'd willingly give up my last few coins
this minute in return for the great pleasure
of punching this buffoon hard on the nose.

CLÉANTE: (*Quietly, to* ORGON)
Don't spoil everything.

DAMIS: But this is unheard-of,
my knuckles itch, you'd better hold me back.

DORINE: You've such a good broad back, Monsieur
Loyal,
a really good hiding might suit you nicely.

M. LOYAL: That kind of talk is actionable, dear,
women are liable to prosecution,
like anybody else.

CLÉANTE: Right, that's enough;
give us your piece of paper and be off.

M. LOYAL: I'll see you very soon. God bless you all!

ORGON: And may He damn you and the man who sent
you!

ORGON, CLÉANTE, MARIANE, ELMIRE, MADAME PERNELLE, DORINE,
DAMIS.

ORGON: Well, mother, am I right? Look at this writ.
                  Now do you understand that he's a traitor?
MME PERNELLE: I'm thunderstruck and discombobulated.
DORINE: (*To* ORGON)
                  I think you're being rather hard on him,
                  this is a confirmation of his goodness,
                  the final proof of his love for his neighbour:
                  he knows that money frequently corrupts,
                  and purely out of charity he wants
                  to take away this threat to your salvation.
ORGON: Be quiet: how many more times must I tell
                                                        you?
CLÉANTE: Come on, now, let's go and discuss the options.
ELMIRE: If you were to expose his insolence,
                  surely the contract would be declared null;
                  his treachery would be seen as too black
                  for him to be allowed to profit by it.

SCENE SIX

VALÈRE, ORGON, CLÉANTE, ELMIRE, MARIANE, MADAME PERNELLE,
DAMIS, DORINE.

VALÈRE: I'm sorry to impose on you like this;
                  an urgent danger made me feel obliged to.
                  A very close friend of mind, who's aware
                  of my connection with you, for my sake,

82

has breached the confidentiality
owed to the State and passed on information,
which gives you no choice but to run away.
An hour ago, that swine who for so long
has cheated you, denounced you to the King,
and, among other accusations, gave him
a case belonging to an enemy
of the State, whose secrets, he said, you kept,
so neglecting your duty as a subject.
I don't know the exact crime you're accused of;
but orders have gone out for your arrest,
and Tartuffe has been told to come as well
to help the officer who's been sent to fetch you.

CLÉANTE: That's how the traitor's trying to reinforce
his claim to take over all your possessions.

ORGON: It's true, he really is an evil monster!

VALÈRE: The slightest hesitation could be fatal.
Here is a thousand louis I have brought you,
my carriage is waiting for you at the gate.
Don't let's waste time; this is a thunderbolt,
the kind of thing you simply can't escape,
unless you run. I'll take you to a safe place
and stay with you until you've got away.

ORGON: I don't know how to thank you for this
                                  kindness!
I'll have to wait before I can repay you,
and I ask God to help me to express
one day my true gratitude for this rescue.
Goodbye; take care, all of you . . .

CLÉANTE: Hurry up;
we'll try to do whatever's necessary.

AN OFFICER, TARTUFFE, VALÈRE, ORGON, ELMIRE, MARIANE,
CLÉANTE, MADAME PERNELLE, DAMIS, DORINE.

TARTUFFE:	(*Stopping* ORGON) All right, all right, not quite so fast, my friend; it's not so very far to where you're going. in the name of the King you're under arrest.
, ORGON:	You traitor, you've been saving this till last! A criminal, delivering the death-blow, the culmination of all your betrayals.
TARTUFFE:	I am impervious to your insults; I'm trained to be tolerant in the sight of God.
CLÉANTE:	How admirably self-controlled of you.
DAMIS:	How insolently he takes the name of God!
TARTUFFE:	I'm completely unmoved by your resentment, all I'm attempting is to do my duty.
MARIANE:	You think this will enhance your reputation? You believe this is honourable conduct?
TARTUFFE:	Conduct suggested by the power that sent me surely can't help but be exemplary.
ORGON:	Have you forgotten that my charity rescued you from a life of poverty?
TARTUFFE:	No, I am well aware of how you helped me; but my first duty must be to the King; the rightful power of this sacred duty has stifled all the gratitude in my heart; to these commitments I would sacrifice my friends, my wife, my parents or myself.
ELMIRE:	Impostor!
DORINE:	He's so treacherously clever at making use of what we most respect!
CLÉANTE:	But if this sense of duty which drives you

84

and which you're so proud of is so consuming,
how come it held off making its appearance
until he caught you molesting his wife?
Why didn't you think of accusing him
until he felt compelled to throw you out?
He's just made you a gift of all his money,
and I don't bring this up as a red herring;
I just wonder, since you think he's so guilty,
how you could condescend to be his heir.

TARTUFFE: (*To the* OFFICER)
Why don't you put an end to all this whining
and be so good as to obey your orders?

OFFICER: Yes, I suppose I've waited far too long,
and what you say is a timely reminder;
I will obey them: follow me at once,
I'm taking you immediately to prison.

TARTUFFE: Who, me, sir?

OFFICER: Yes, you, sir.

TARTUFFE: But why to prison?

OFFICER: I don't have to explain myself to you.
(*To* ORGON)
Calm yourself, sir. You're living in the reign
of a King who's declared war on deceit,
a King whose eyes can see into your heart,
whom no impostor's cunning can mislead.
The sharp perceptiveness of that great mind
sees everything in its proper perspective.
He's too intelligent to be swayed by passion
or to fall into any kind of excess.
He's always paid tribute to real goodness,
without letting enthusiasm blind him,
and his love for the genuine has never
closed his mind to the horrors of bad faith.
He's seen through more effective traps than this
man set, he never really stood a chance.
His perspicacity discerned at once
the wickedness of this man's secret heart.

He came to denounce you and betrayed
                            himself:
by a supremely fitting stroke of justice,
he let slip something which allowed the King
to identify him as a wanted man,
whose long record, under another name
would fill a book with lists of vicious crimes.
His Majesty also despises his vile
disloyalty and ingratitude to you
in addition to all the other horrors,
and only made me his subordinate
to see how far his shamelessness would go
before we made him make full restitution.
The King wants me to strip him, in your
                           presence,
of all your papers, which he claims to own,
and exercises his prerogative
to break the contract which you signed to give
                           him
all that you own, and finally he pardons
the crime your friend's exile made you commit,
as a reward for your support for him
during the troubles, just to demonstrate
that he knows the time to pay back a favour
is when you least expect it, and that he
cherishes the deserving and prefers
remembering the good to bearing grudges.

DORINE: Thank God!

MME PERNELLE: What a relief.

ELMIRE: A happy end.

MARIANE: Who would have thought it could turn out this
                           way?

(ORGON *turns to* TARTUFFE, *as the* OFFICER *leads him away.*)

ORGON: What about this, then, traitor?

CLÉANTE: No, no, stop it,
don't stoop to mere abuse. Just let him go,

poor wretch, to his unhappy fate, and don't
add to the guilt which must be crippling him.
Better to hope this may encourage him
to return gladly to the paths of virtue,
to turn against his evil and repent
and cause our great King to temper his justice.
Meanwhile, you must go on your knees to him
and show how grateful you are for his lenience.

ORGON: That's well said, yes. Let's go and kiss his feet
and praise him for the goodness of his heart;
and that duty acquitted, we must meet
another necessary obligation
and reward a sincere and generous love
by celebrating your wedding, Valère.

FAVORITE
BROADWAY COMEDIES
from
SAMUEL FRENCH, INC.

BAREFOOT IN THE PARK – BEDROOM FARCE –
BLITHE SPIRIT – BUTTERFLIES ARE FREE –
CALIFORNIA SUITE – CHAMPAGNE COMPLEX –
CHAPTER TWO – COME BLOW YOUR HORN – DA –
THE GINGERBREAD LADY – GOD'S FAVORITE –
THE GOOD DOCTOR – HAPPY BIRTHDAY,
WANDA JUNE – HAY FEVER – HOW THE OTHER
HALF LOVES – I OUGHT TO BE IN PICTURES –
JUMPERS – KNOCK KNOCK – LAST OF THE RED
HOT LOVERS – MY FAT FRIEND – NEVER TOO LATE
– NIGHT AND DAY – THE NORMAN CONQUESTS –
NORMAN, IS THAT YOU? – THE ODD COUPLE –
OTHERWISE ENGAGED – THE OWL AND THE
PUSSYCAT – THE PRISONER OF 2ND AVENUE –
THE PRIVATE EAR AND THE PUBLIC EYE –
THE RAINMAKER – SAME TIME, NEXT YEAR –
THE SHOW OFF – 6 RMS RIV VU – THE SUNSHINE
BOYS – A THOUSAND CLOWNS – TRAVESTIES –
TWIGS – TWO FOR THE SEASAW

*For descriptions of these and all our plays, consult our Basic
Catalogue of Plays.*